THE 10

Most Memorable Speeches in American History

Hughena Matheson

Series Editor
Jeffrey D. Wilhelm

Much thought, debate, and research went into choosing and ranking the 10 items in each book in this series. We realize that everyone has his or her own opinion of what is most significant, revolutionary, amazing, deadly, and so on. As you read, you may agree with our choices, or you may be surprised — and that's the way it should be!

an imprint of

www.scholastic.com/librarypublishing

A Rubicon book published in association with Scholastic Inc.

Ru'bĭcon © 2007 Rubicon Publishing Inc.
www.rubiconpublishing.com

Associate Publishers: Kim Koh, Miriam Bardswich
Project Editor: Amy Land
Editor: Bettina Fehrenbach
Editorial Assistant: Jessica Rose
Project Manager/Designer: Jeanette MacLean
Graphic Designers: Gabriela Castillo, Jeanette MacLean

The publisher gratefully acknowledges the following for permission to reprint copyrighted material in this book.

Every reasonable effort has been made to trace the owners of copyrighted material and to make due acknowledgment. Any errors or omissions drawn to our attention will be gladly rectified in future editions.

"Inspiration for America," excerpt from a memoir by John Coyne. Reprinted with permission.

"Reagan speechwriter offers high praise for ex-president at forum," by Cecilia Keehan, from *Los Altos Town Crier*, January 28, 2004. © 2004 *Los Altos Town Crier*. Used with permission.

Cover image: Martin Luther King, Jr.–National Archives, istockphoto

Library and Archives Canada Cataloguing in Publication

Matheson, Hughena
        The 10 most memorable speeches in American history/Hughena Matheson.

ISBN 978-1-55448-478-2

        1. Readers (Elementary). 2. Readers—Speeches, addresses, etc.—
History. I. Title. II. Title: Ten most memorable speeches in American history.

PE1117.M38 2007   428.6   C2007-904045-4

1 2 3 4 5 6 7 8 9 10   10   16 15 14 13 12 11 10 09 08 07

Printed in Singapore

Contents

6

26

38

Hear! Hear!

Have you ever heard a speech that was so powerful it moved you to tears, motivated you to do something, or inspired you to set higher goals?

The spoken word can have enormous power. A well-written speech delivered by a good speaker can stir up strong emotions in listeners. That is why so many successful politicians, leaders, and social activists are great speakers. They are able to convince their listeners to believe in their dreams and goals, and to take action with them.

In this book, we present what we think are the 10 most memorable speeches in American history. In making our selections, we took into consideration the importance of the message and the impact it had on America and, sometimes, the world. We also noted how eloquent the speech was; if it convinced listeners to take action or calmed them; how it influenced history; and how it brought about significant change in thought and action.

Michael Waldman, a speechwriter for former President Bill Clinton, described a great speech as one in which "the moment, the message, and the messenger come together as one." He could have been talking about all 10 speeches in this book!

---

eloquent: *uses forceful or impressive language*

What is the most memorable speech in American history?

"AN HISTORIC

This is an histori

— for the Cong

moment

Nancy Pelosi is one of the most powerful women in American politics.

MOMENT ..."

WHO: Nancy Pelosi, Speaker of the U.S. House of Representatives

WHERE AND WHEN: Swearing-in ceremony, House of Representatives, Washington, D.C., January 4, 2007

SIGNIFICANCE: First female Speaker in American history

History was made on January 4, 2007. This was the day when the United States House of Representatives elected its first female Speaker, Nancy Pelosi.

The Speaker is the leader of the House of Representatives. It is a very important role. Among other duties, the Speaker decides which issues should be presented and discussed in the House. As Speaker, Pelosi is second in line for the presidency. This means that, should anything happen to the president and the vice president, she becomes president.

In her acceptance speech, Pelosi stated: "This is an historic moment — for the Congress, and for the women of America. It is a moment for which we have waited for over 200 years."

Pelosi stressed the significance of her election for American women: "For our daughters and grand-daughters, today we have broken the marble ceiling. For our daughters and our granddaughters now, the sky is the limit." When Nancy Pelosi spoke of breaking the "marble ceiling," she was referring to the popular phrase "breaking through the glass ceiling." This phrase refers to women no longer being held back because of their gender. Because the ceiling of the Capitol Building is marble, Pelosi's rewording has added significance for the future of women in politics.

"AN HISTORIC MOMENT ..."

THE SPEAKER

Nancy D'Alesandro was born into a political family. Her father was a member of Congress and her brother became a mayor. After graduating from Trinity College in Washington, D.C., she married Paul Pelosi and moved with him to San Francisco. When the youngest of their five children started school, Nancy Pelosi became involved in politics.

THE MOMENT

Nancy Pelosi made this speech on the day she was sworn in as Speaker of the House. Loud cheers and applause echoed around the room as she stated what the historic moment represented: "Hope, hope, that is what America is about and it is in that spirit that I was sent to Congress. And today, I thank my colleagues. By electing me Speaker, you have brought us closer to the ideal of equality that is America's heritage and America's hope."

heritage: *birthright*

? What do you think Nancy Pelosi means in the last sentence? Restate her hope in your own words.

THE IMPACT

As the first woman in this powerful position, Nancy Pelosi has opened the door for women to move into other important roles in government. In her opening remarks, Pelosi outlined the six items she wished Congress to pursue within the "first 100 hours" of her term. Her aim was to improve the life of the average American. The first four items were passed in the first 100 hours she was in office. The last two were passed a week later.

? Find out about the six items on Pelosi's list. Research the changes that came about as a result of the bills passed by the 110th Congress.

The Expert Says...

" 'Failure is impossible' predicted suffragette Susan B. Anthony [who was] fighting for women's right to vote. One hundred years later, her words came true as Congresswoman Nancy Pelosi became Speaker of the U.S. House of Representatives. "

— Dr. M.G. Slavenas, Professor of Modern Languages, Canisius College

Nancy Pelosi is handed the gavel during a swearing-in ceremony in the chamber of the House of Representatives, 2007.

10

9   8   7   6

Political Milestones for American Women

Nancy Pelosi's election as Speaker of the House now leaves only two political mountains for women to climb: vice president and president. The profiles below describe other women's firsts in government.

Jeannette Rankin
In 1916, Rankin was the first woman to be elected to the House of Representatives.

Hattie Wyatt Caraway
In 1931, Caraway was the first woman elected to the Senate.

Sandra Day O'Connor
In 1981, O'Connor took her seat as the first female judge to serve on the Supreme Court.

Geraldine Ferraro
In 1984, Ferraro was the first woman nominated by a major party to run for vice president.

?
Who will be the first female American president?

Take Note
The election of Nancy Pelosi as the first female Speaker of the House was a historic event. Pelosi earns the #10 spot on our list for making history and for her powerful words and actions.
• Why do you think it took so long for a woman to become the Speaker of the House of Representatives?

5   4   3   2   1

President John F. Kennedy making his inauguration speech from the balcony of the Capitol Building in Washington, D.C.

LOW AMERICANS ...”

WHO: John Fitzgerald Kennedy, president, 1961–1963

WHERE AND WHEN: Inaugural Address, Washington, D.C., January 20, 1961

SIGNIFICANCE: Kennedy's words inspired Americans to serve their country.

On a cold winter day in 1961, John F. Kennedy took to the podium on the steps of the Capitol Building. Americans listened spellbound as the young president delivered his inaugural address.

Kennedy wanted to win the confidence of Americans with his inaugural speech. And he hoped to inspire young Americans to think beyond themselves. He delivered a short speech filled with noble ideals.

As the first president born in the 20th century, Kennedy noted that a younger generation was now in charge: “[T]he torch has been passed ... to a generation born in this [20th] century.”

He spoke to the developing countries, and pledged “our best efforts to help them help themselves ...”

He promised to work for a world in which “the strong are just ... and the weak secure ... and the peace preserved.”

Then in the climax of his speech, he challenged Americans: “And so, my fellow Americans, ask not what your country can do for you; ask what you can do for your country.” The sentence inspired all Americans, and continues to do so today, more than 40 years later.

---

inaugural address: *speech by a president on the first day in office*
just: *guided by truth and fairness*

"AND SO, MY FELLOW AMERICANS..."

THE SPEAKER

John Fitzgerald Kennedy (1917 – 1963) was born into a wealthy and politically active family. After graduating from Harvard, he joined the navy and was awarded a medal for heroism in World War II. Kennedy began his political career as a member of Congress and then was elected a senator. In November 1960, he was elected president, the youngest in American history.

Just 1,000 days into his presidency, John F. Kennedy was assassinated in Dallas. In his short presidency, he had left an unforgettable legacy.

THE MOMENT

When Kennedy made his inaugural speech in 1961, America was at war in Vietnam and in the midst of a Cold War with the Soviet Union. Kennedy delivered a strong message clearly indicating that he valued liberty: "Let every nation know … we shall pay any price, bear any burden, meet any hardship, support any friend, oppose any foe to assure the survival of liberty."

legacy: *gift; something handed down*
Cold War: *period of hostile relations between the former Soviet Union and the United States, from the late 1940s until the end of the 1980s*

THE IMPACT

Americans responded wholeheartedly to Kennedy's challenge. Thousands of young Americans traveled to different parts of the world as members of the Peace Corps to help people in developing countries.

Kennedy's promise of peace at "any price" was tested in October 1962 when the Soviet Union set up missiles in Cuba. Kennedy demanded that the Soviets remove the missiles, and ordered a naval blockade of Cuba. The Soviets backed down — and Kennedy saved the day.

blockade: *measure to isolate an enemy country by preventing supplies from entering it*

Ask someone who lived through the events of the Cuban Missile Crisis how he or she felt at the time. How was the person affected by this event?

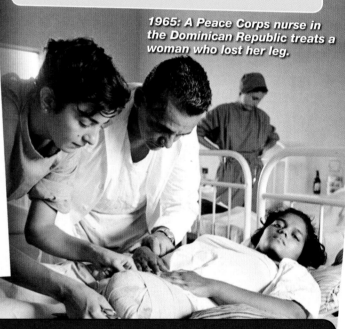

1965: A Peace Corps nurse in the Dominican Republic treats a woman who lost her leg.

Quick Fact

During World War II, Kennedy was awarded a medal after his PT boat was hit by a Japanese destroyer. He led the survivors safely to an island not far from where their ship was hit.

The Expert Says...

"Kennedy's call to get involved reflects his own hope in the future and his belief in the worth of each individual. It found a special echo among young people by inspiring them to join the Peace Corps and become America's goodwill ambassadors.

— Dr. Julius Slavenas, Professor of History, Buffalo State College

Inspiration for America

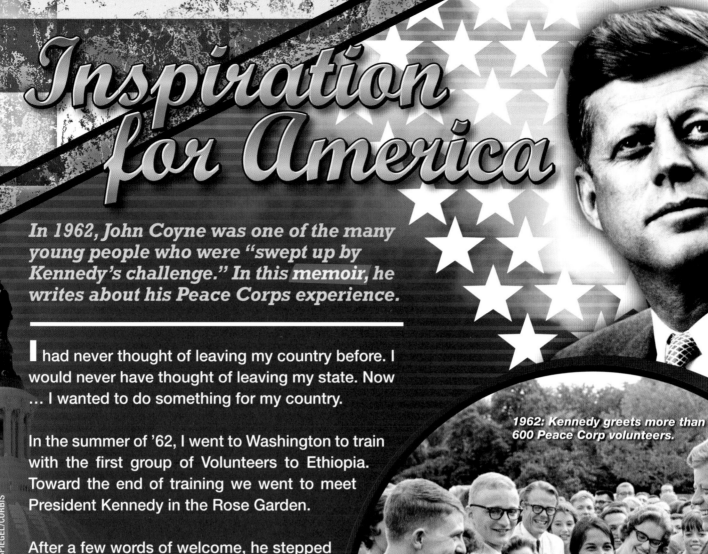

In 1962, John Coyne was one of the many young people who were "swept up by Kennedy's challenge." In this **memoir**, he writes about his Peace Corps experience.

I had never thought of leaving my country before. I would never have thought of leaving my state. Now … I wanted to do something for my country.

In the summer of '62, I went to Washington to train with the first group of Volunteers to Ethiopia. Toward the end of training we went to meet President Kennedy in the Rose Garden.

After a few words of welcome, he stepped down to shake hands and wish us well. And as he turned to leave he stopped and asked us to write, to tell him how it was going, and then he grinned and added, "But no post cards." …

Our service overseas was often silent and often went unheralded. Some of the bridges we built did not stand, a few of the schools where we taught are now closed … We were seldom as successful as we had hoped.

But the Peace Corps took us out of America, cut us loose from these shores, and taught us how to be citizens of the world. Because of the Peace Corps all of us are forever changed.

unheralded: unnoticed

1962: Kennedy greets more than 600 Peace Corp volunteers.

Take Note

John F. Kennedy's inaugural speech is #9 on our list. While it did not mark a breakthrough moment in American history, as Nancy Pelosi's speech did, Kennedy's inspirational speech motivated Americans to try to make their country and the world a better place. More than 40 years later, his words continue to inspire Americans.

• President Kennedy encouraged Americans to give service to their country. Today, some schools require students to do community service as a requirement for graduation. Do you agree with this policy, or do you think community service should be voluntary? Give reasons for your answer.

Terrell, a high-school teacher and principal, was the first African American woman to be appointed to the District of Columbia Board of Education.

ED WOMAN ..."

WHO: Mary Church Terrell, civil and women's rights activist

WHERE AND WHEN: United Women's Club, Washington, D.C., October 10, 1906

SIGNIFICANCE: Terrell raised awareness of discrimination against African Americans in the nation's capital.

"**A**s a colored woman I might enter Washington any night, a stranger in a strange land, and walk miles without finding a place to lay my head."

With these poignant words, Mary Church Terrell, a civil rights activist, highlighted the fact that more than 40 years after the end of the Civil War, African Americans still faced discrimination. And this was 60 years before the civil rights movement.

Terrell went on to provide another example of the discrimination she faced: "As a colored woman I may walk from the Capitol to the White House ... without finding a single restaurant in which I would be permitted to take a morsel of food, if it was patronized by white people, unless I were willing to sit behind a screen."

And then she described what was the worst thing about all this racist behavior: "And surely nowhere in the world do oppression [cruelty] and persecution [harassment] based solely on the color of the skin appear more hateful and hideous than in the capital of the United States ..."

Mary Church Terrell made people aware of the need for action to end discrimination in the U.S. in the 20th century.

---

poignant: *moving*
morsel: *small piece*
patronized: *visited*

Why do you think Terrell felt it was especially bad that she was facing discrimination in the nation's capital?

"AS A COLORED WOMAN ..."

THE SPEAKER

Mary Church Terrell (1863 – 1954) was born the year President Abraham Lincoln issued the Emancipation Proclamation, calling for the freedom of slaves in the South. Both of Terrell's parents were former slaves who later became very wealthy through the buying and selling of real estate. Terrell was one of the first African American women to earn a bachelor's degree from Oberlin College in Ohio. An educator, writer, and public speaker, Terrell spent her life fighting for equal rights for women and African Americans.

THE MOMENT

Mary Church Terrell made her famous speech in 1906 at a meeting of the United Women's Club in Washington, D.C. She showed that no matter how qualified African Americans were, they were still denied equal and fair treatment.

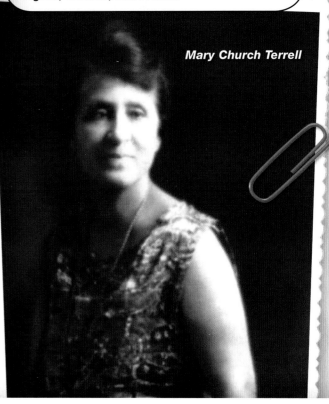

Mary Church Terrell

? Why do you think perfectly qualified African Americans were denied jobs? How much do you think things have changed? What types of discrimination remain today? Explain your answers.

The Expert Says...

" In public life and in ... society no woman of the race has commanded more attention from the American and the international public than Mary Church Terrell. "

— Benjamin Griffith Brawley (1882-1939), educator and author

THE IMPACT

Terrell's speech made people aware of the terrible discrimination in America. A lifelong activist, Terrell fought for, and won, many important civil rights for African Americans and women. In 1909, she was a founding member of NAACP (the National Association for the Advancement of Colored People). During World War I, she helped with the demobilization of African American military personnel. She worked in the suffrage movement that fought for women's right to vote.

At the age of 80, when most people are retired, Terrell succeeded in persuading the local chapter of the National Association of University Women to admit African American members. And at the age of 87, she won a court ruling that forced restaurants to desegregate.

demobilization: *release from military service*
desegregate: *stop separating races*

COLORED

WAITING ROOM

A Fight for Rights

The end of the Civil War marked the end of slavery, but it did not stop racial discrimination in the United States. This article describes how Mary Church Terrell won a major battle against the segregated restaurants in Washington, D.C.

In 1872 and 1873, anti-discrimination laws were passed in Washington, D.C. One law stated that all restaurants had "to serve any respectable, well-behaved person regardless of color, or face a $1,000 fine and forfeiture of their license." Unfortunately, these laws were left out when new laws were written in the 1890s.

In 1950, at the age of 87, Mary Church Terrell started a campaign to have the anti-discrimination laws reinstated. She began by targeting Thompson Restaurant, a segregated restaurant. Terrell and her colleagues went to the restaurant for a meal. When the restaurant refused to serve them, the group filed a lawsuit against it. It took three years for the court to arrive at a decision. In the meantime, Terrell turned her attention on other restaurants. She organized boycotts, picketing, and sit-ins. Finally, in June 1953, Terrell won. The court ruled that segregated restaurants in Washington, D.C., were illegal.

forfeiture: *loss*
reinstated: *put back*
boycotts: *refusals to buy, sell, or use*

Quick Fact

Terrell's autobiography, *A Colored Woman in a White World*, published in 1940, is the first full-length autobiography by an African American woman.

A woman bars the way as protesters are about to enter a segregated lunch counter.

Take Note

Mary Church Terrell's speech marches into the #8 spot. While President Kennedy inspired a nation with his speech, Terrell raised awareness that racial discrimination was a terrible part of life in the U.S. — even in the 20th century, and right in the nation's capital! She made people realize the urgent need to take action to wipe out racism.
• How can individuals help stop discrimination based on race, gender, beliefs, or dress?

5   4   3   2   1

Franklin D. Roosevelt was the first president to appear on television when he opened the New York World's Fair in 1939.

ING ...."

WHO: Franklin Delano Roosevelt, president, 1933–1945

WHERE AND WHEN: Inaugural Address, Washington, D.C., March 4, 1933

SIGNIFICANCE: Roosevelt's speech lifted the American people out of their despair over the Great Depression.

Franklin D. Roosevelt became president during one of the most difficult times in American history.

The Great Depression, which began in 1929 and lasted through the 1930s, was a time of extreme poverty in America. Banks and businesses went bankrupt. Millions of Americans did not have jobs. Farmers lost their family farms. Homeowners lost their homes. Starving families lined up at soup kitchens. Across the country, people were overcome by fear. They felt desperate and hopeless.

In his inaugural address, Franklin D. Roosevelt delivered a serious speech designed to calm the American people and to offer them hope. With confidence, he stated: "This great Nation will endure as it has endured, will revive, and will prosper." He went on to rally the spirits of the people with these memorable words: "So first of all let me assert my firm belief that the only thing we have to fear is fear itself."

Roosevelt's stirring words and confidence lifted Americans out of their despair. He laid out a plan of action that eventually restored America's economy to prosperity.

endure: *get through hardship*
prosper: *achieve economic success*

"THE ONLY THING ..."

THE SPEAKER

Franklin D. Roosevelt was born in 1882, the only child of wealthy parents. His father taught him that being wealthy meant he had a responsibility to help those who were not so lucky.

Roosevelt entered politics as a way to serve the people. In 1910, he became a senator in New York. In 1921, he was struck with polio, a disease that can cause paralysis. Roosevelt fought hard to regain his health, but he would never walk again. This did not stop his political career. In 1928, he was elected governor of New York. Four years later, he won the presidential election.

THE MOMENT

Roosevelt delivered his powerful inaugural speech in the midst of the worst days of the Great Depression. He knew Americans needed to be comforted. Recognizing the "dark realities of the moment," he declared war on the Depression. "I shall ask the Congress for ... broad Executive power to wage a war against the emergency, as great as the power that would be given to me if we were in fact invaded by a foreign foe."

Millions of people listened to the speech over the radio. They rallied to Roosevelt's promises for a better future.

THE IMPACT

Within days of his inauguration, Roosevelt called a special session of Congress. He proposed his New Deal — a program for change aimed at pulling America out of the Depression. Just 100 days later, Roosevelt's New Deal provided millions of people with jobs, hope, and dignity.

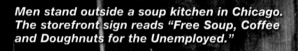

Men stand outside a soup kitchen in Chicago. The storefront sign reads "Free Soup, Coffee and Doughnuts for the Unemployed."

The Expert Says...

" Roosevelt knew that recovery partly depended on the people's faith in the political and economic system, and this began his effort to restore that faith. "

— David W. Rohde, Professor of Political Science and Director of the Political Institutions, Duke University

? How do you think people's faith in the economy helps it to grow and succeed?

This is one of the few known photographs of Roosevelt in a wheelchair. He didn't want the American people to see him affected by his ailment.

A Letter to the Roosevelts

Millions of Americans were grateful to Roosevelt for his New Deal. He received many thank-you letters. Read the letter below from one farming family in Minnesota that had suffered during the Depression but had not lost their home.

TO PRESIDENT AND MRS. F.D. ROOSEVELT
AUGUST 10, 1934
THE WHITE HOUSE, WASHINGTON, D.C.
DEAR FRIENDS:

This is a letter of thanks. Owing to the president's kindness in referring a letter (we wrote you last December, 1932) to the Federal Farm Credit Administration ... we are still in possession of our home — and have a Federal Land Bank Commissioners loan of $1200. ...

We asked in our former letter if the refinancing program was only for the big farmers — that seemed to us the way it was being applied here, — but we know now that it means others too, and the "New Deal" means something to us. ...

We are much interested in the building plans of the government and in the new homes being built. We know how happy the families housed in them will be. ...

... I did want you folks down there to know that your efforts are helping people, helping people to help themselves. Here's one grateful family in Clearwater, Minnesota, who owe you many thanks and appreciation. ...

With every good wish for your health and happiness and every appreciation of all the help you are trying to give to those who need it so badly. We are sincerely your friends.

I.O. Arney and family

Quick Fact

Roosevelt is the only president to serve four terms. After his death, the 22nd Amendment, stating presidents could not be elected to more than two terms, was passed.

Take Note

President Roosevelt's inaugural speech reached out to Americans during a devastating time in their lives. Americans were relieved to know that someone strong was in charge, and that he had a plan to help end their troubles. His memorable words of encouragement and hope ring in at #7 on our list.

• Roosevelt communicated with Americans regularly in radio addresses known as "fireside chats." Through these chats, he explained his programs and encouraged the American people. What do you think about this idea? Should all presidents participate in this type of program? Why or why not?

"THE AMERICAN

In 1984, Jordan was voted "Best Living Orator" and elected to the Texas Women's Hall of Fame.

BARBARA JORDAN–© BETTMANN/CORBIS

DREAM IS NOT DEAD."

WHO: Barbara Jordan, Member of Congress and Professor

WHERE AND WHEN: Keynote address, at Democratic National Convention, New York City, July 13, 1992

SIGNIFICANCE: Jordan's powerful message in an election year helped bring national attention to the challenges the poor and minorities face.

During the 1980s and the early 1990s, the United States experienced a period of recession. Many people lost their jobs and homes. The recession was a major issue during the 1992 presidential election.

Barbara Jordan was invited by Bill Clinton to speak at the 1992 Democratic National Convention. A dynamic speaker, Jordan focused on the problems of the poor and the minorities in the country. She urged the American people to help improve the status of the homeless and the unemployed.

Jordan told her audience that "the American Dream is not dead. It is not dead. It is gasping for breath, but it is not dead." She went on to say that "the American Dream is slipping away from too many black and brown mothers and their children … from the homeless of every color of every sex. It's slipping away from those immigrants living in communities without water and sewer systems."

In her speech, Jordan also addressed women's issues. She felt that because women made up half of the American population, they should share the same opportunities as men. "This country can ill afford to continue to function using less than half of its human resources, brainpower, and kinetic energy."

recession: *extended slowdown in business activity*
kinetic: *active; dynamic*

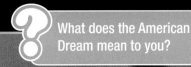

? What does the American Dream mean to you?

"THE AMERICAN DREAM IS NOT DEAD."

THE SPEAKER

Barbara Jordan (1936–1996) was born to a poor Texas family during segregation. Jordan did well in school and found she had a gift for public speaking. In 1952, she won first place in the Texas State Ushers Oratorical Contest. Jordan's love of speaking turned into an interest in law. She attended Boston University Law School and was one of two African American women to graduate in 1959.

Jordan was elected to the Texas House of Representatives in 1966 and became the first African American woman to hold the position of senator in Texas. In 1972, she was elected to the U.S. House of Representatives. After retiring from politics in 1979, Jordan became a professor at the University of Texas.

segregation: *separation of a race, class, or group*
oratorical: *public speaking*

Quick Fact

Both the Democratic and the Republican parties hold a convention every four years, usually a few months before the presidential election. Party delegates from all 50 states attend. The main objective is to nominate the party's candidates to run for president and vice president and to establish a platform of issues on which the party would focus.

The Expert Says...

"And just as young Barbara Jordan listened to the words of [John F. Kennedy] and was 'bit by the bug' of politics, so did she go on to inspire another generation of young leaders when she took the podium at the 1992 Democratic Convention."

— Barbara Boxer, Senator of California

Barbara Jordan, circa 1976

THE MOMENT

In 1992, Jordan was the keynote speaker at the Democratic National Convention. Jordan spoke about poverty and unequal opportunities for minorities. She was able to convince her listeners to embrace all Americans. "We are one, we Americans. We're one and we reject any intruder who seeks to divide us on the basis of race and color. ... Our strength in this country is rooted in our diversity."

THE IMPACT

Jordan's passionate speech echoed throughout the election campaign. Her call for change and for improvement in the economy were themes that Bill Clinton and Al Gore emphasized in the months leading up to the election.

Barbara Jordan's
Keynote Address

Barbara Jordan eloquently stated the need for change in politics. This excerpt from her 1992 keynote address shows her way with words.

"... We will change in order to satisfy the present, in order to satisfy the future — but we will not die. We will change, but we will not die. ... When the economy is growing and we are taking care of our air and soil and water, we all prosper. And we can do all of that. ...

I will tell you the kind of economy I'm talking about. ... I mean an economy where a young black woman or man from the Fifth Ward in Houston or South Central Los Angeles, or a young person in the colonias of the lower Rio Grande Valley — I'm talking about an economy where those persons can go to a public school, learn the skills that will enable her or him to prosper.

We must have an economy that does not force that migrant worker's child to miss school for a full day so that she can work at less than the minimum wage — and doing that the family can still only afford one meal a day. ...

One overdue change, which you have already heard a lot about, is already underway. And that is reflected in the number of women now challenging the councils of political power. These women are challenging those councils of political power because they have been dominated by white, male policy makers and that is wrong. That horizon of gender equity is limitless for us. And what we see today is simply a dress rehearsal for the day and time we meet in convention to nominate Madame President. ...

---

colonias: *Mexican or Mexican American settlements on the U.S. border*

horizon: *possibility*

? After reading her speech, do you agree that Barbara Jordan is an eloquent speaker? Explain.

Quick Fact

Barbara Jordan also gave the keynote address at the 1976 Democratic National Convention. She was the first woman and the first African American to do this.

Take Note

Barbara Jordan takes the #6 spot on our list. Her eloquent speech — that change was necessary — provided a powerful message to the American people. Jordan continues to be an inspiration to many Americans long after her death.
- It is more than 15 years since Barbara Jordan delivered her speech. Do you think the changes she was calling for have taken place in the U.S.? Go online to find information to help you arrive at a decision.

5   4   3   2   1

PRESIDENT RONALD REAGAN AT THE BRANDENBURG GATE IN WEST BERLIN—© CORBIS

ACHTUNG!
SIE VERLASSEN
JETZT
WEST BERLIN

Before the Berlin Wall was built, 10,000 people a week were leaving East Germany. They wanted a better life in prosperous and democratic West Germany.

THIS WALL!"

WHO: Ronald Reagan, president, 1981–1989

WHERE AND WHEN: Brandenburg Gate at the Berlin Wall, West Berlin, Germany, June 12, 1987

SIGNIFICANCE: Historians believe that this speech helped speed the end of communism in Eastern Europe.

Imagine having a wall built through the center of your city. The Wall is topped with barbed wire and booby-trapped with explosives. Armed guards shoot if anyone tries to escape. How would this captivity make you feel? For nearly 30 years, East Germans were held behind such a wall — the Berlin Wall.

At the end of World War II, Germany was divided into two — East Germany came under communist rule while West Germany was a democratic republic. In 1961, the East German government, with the support of the Soviet Union, built the Berlin Wall to prevent East Germans from leaving for West Germany.

In the 1980s, Mikhail Gorbachev, Premier of the Soviet Union, began to reform Soviet policies. However, Ronald Reagan thought these freedoms were coming too slowly. On a visit to the Wall in 1987, with all of Germany listening, he took the chance to make his point. The former actor declared: "General Secretary Gorbachev, if you seek peace, if you seek prosperity for the Soviet Union and Eastern Europe, if you seek liberalization: Come here to this gate! Mr. Gorbachev, open this gate! Mr. Gorbachev, tear down this wall!"

Historians mark this speech as an important event in helping speed the end of communism in Eastern Europe. Gorbachev began to reform Soviet policies introducing *glasnost*, or openness.

"TEAR DOWN THIS WALL!"

Quick Fact

The Berlin Wall was 96 miles long and made up of two parallel walls. The "death strip" between the two walls was covered with gravel, making it easy to see footprints. Armed guards kept watch and had orders to shoot those trying to escape.

THE SPEAKER

Ronald Reagan (1911–2004) was a Hollywood actor before he turned to politics. In 1966, he was elected governor of California, where he served for two terms. In 1980, Reagan was elected president. Known as "the great communicator," Reagan was a popular president. He worked on his campaign promise to restore "the great, confident roar of American progress and optimism." He was a strong opponent of communism. He once described the Soviet Union and its allies as "the evil empire."

? Like Arnold Schwarzenegger, Reagan was governor of California. Do you think most people take actors seriously when they enter politics? Why or why not?

THE MOMENT

Reagan was in Berlin for the 750th anniversary of its founding. He delivered this speech on the West side of the Berlin Wall in front of the Brandenburg Gate. Thousands of Berliners, on both the East and West sides, listened to the speech. Reagan compared the prosperous democratic West Germany with the struggling communist East Germany and concluded, "Freedom leads to prosperity. … Freedom is the victor." Then Reagan challenged Gorbachev to "tear down this wall."

THE IMPACT

Reagan's speech in 1987 provided a great push for the movement for freedom in Eastern Europe. On November 9, 1989, the Wall came down, and Germany was one country again. Former East Germans had a chance for a new life, and families were reunited.

Quick Fact

The Brandenburg Gate was opened on December 22, 1989, about a month after the Wall came down. The public destroyed the Wall over a period of weeks. Many people have chunks of the Wall as souvenirs.

A demonstrator pounds away at the Berlin Wall at the East German border. Guards look on from above at the Brandenburg Gate.

The Expert Says...

"He [Reagan] understood that words could bring the country together, and he was always looking for ways to give voice to a special time and place."

— Kenneth T. Walsh, *U.S. News & World Report*

10   9   8   7   6

Town Crier

Reagan speechwriter offers high praise for ex-president at forum

BY CECILIA KEEHAN, SPECIAL TO THE *LOS ALTOS TOWN CRIER*, JANUARY 28, 2004

It wasn't an easy decision on Reagan's part to say these controversial words, "Mr. Gorbachev, tear down this wall." As you read this newspaper article, you'll learn that Reagan had a little help ...

As soon as Reagan was scheduled to speak in Berlin with the Brandenburg Gate behind him, Peter Robinson [Reagan's speechwriter] began working on the speech. He met with a group of Berliners over dinner and asked them whether they had gotten used to the Wall. One of the guests said that his sister lived only a few kilometers [just over a mile] from the Wall but they could not communicate. The hostess said that if Soviet General Secretary Mikhail Gorbachev was serious about perestroika, he would come to Berlin and prove it.

Robinson wrote the president's single most effective and confrontational line in Reagan's historic address at the Berlin Wall, when he called upon Gorbachev to "tear down this wall."

The writer said that the speech had been submitted to "staffing" and virtually the entire White House apparatus had spoken up against it.

Knowing that the speech would be heard not only in West Berlin, but in the East as well, Robinson said it was imperative that the sensitive line be spoken — but the decision had to be the president's.

In Berlin, the president met with his speechwriter and made the final decision. The president said, "Although the boys at State are going to kill me, it is the right thing to do," and the phrase "tear down this wall" was spoken. The rest is history. ...

---

perestroika: *Russian term for reconstructing; Gorbachev used it to describe his political and economic reforms*
apparatus: *organization*
imperative: *very important*
State: *State Department that handles foreign affairs*

Take Note

Ronald Reagan's speech is ranked #5 on our list. His words were a powerful symbol to the people of East Germany. The Wall was literally torn down two years after his speech.
• What skills do you think actors have that would make them good politicians? What skills do politicians have that might make them great actors?

5   4   3   2   1

Gore was one of the first politicians to grasp the seriousness of climate change. He held the first congressional hearings on the subject in the late 1970s.

RAL ISSUE ..."

WHO: Al Gore, environmental activist, former vice president, 1992–2000

WHERE AND WHEN: New York University School of Law, Policy Address, September 18, 2006

SIGNIFICANCE: Gore alerted the world to the seriousness of global warming.

"This is a moral issue — it affects the survival of human civilization."

Al Gore was one of the first politicians to study the effects of global warming and to warn the government and businesses about it. Global warming is the gradual increase in Earth's temperature. Global warming is caused by the production of greenhouse gases. Since the early 2000s, Gore has been traveling around the nation speaking about the urgent need to take action against global warming. He has made global warming an important topic of discussion and concern.

In this speech to the students of the New York University School of Law, Gore stressed that it was the responsibility of everyone to help slow down global warming: "Put simply, it is wrong to destroy the habitability of our planet and ruin the prospects of every generation that follows ours."

He offered suggestions for ways to reduce greenhouse gases and become environmentally friendly. And he emphasized the need for America to take the lead in this process: "Simply put, in order for the world to respond urgently to the climate crisis, the United States must lead the way."

greenhouse gases: *gases such as carbon dioxide that produce a greenhouse or warming effect in the atmosphere*
habitability: *suitability for living*

"THIS IS A MORAL ISSUE..."

In 2006, Al Gore presented his findings on global warming in a documentary film titled An Inconvenient Truth. It won two Oscars and has received a lot of praise since its release.

THE SPEAKER

Gore was born into a political family. His father served in the House of Representatives, and his mother was one of the first women to graduate from Vanderbilt University Law School. He served his time in the Vietnam War as an army reporter. He was vice president of the U.S. for eight years when Bill Clinton was president. He narrowly lost the 2000 election to George W. Bush.

? If Al Gore became president, do you think he could focus as much attention on global warming? Why or why not?

The Expert Says...

"The culture of Washington, D.C., is: 'Don't do anything unless there is a crisis.' And that's been the problem with global warming for all these years ... Al Gore has realized that if you want to get attention, you really have to focus on the crisis.

— Richard Harris, National Public Radio Science Correspondent

THE MOMENT

Al Gore spoke to students of NYU and presented new approaches that the government could take to lower the rate at which greenhouse gases are released into the atmosphere. He also challenged America to take bold new steps in preventing global warming.

THE IMPACT

With his film, speeches, and continued efforts, Gore has raised awareness of global warming around the world. For years, it has been a serious issue, but Gore has contributed to the general acceptance that global warming exists. As a result, there is hope for governments to make changes in environmental policies and for individuals to take action. Gore calls for a plan, starting with a reduction in carbon emissions from cars and factories and going on to building energy-efficient homes, and getting people to do simple things at home such as using less hot water and turning off electronic devices that are not in use.

? What steps can you and your family take in your community to help prevent global warming from becoming a bigger problem?

As glaciers melt, animals that live in polar regions are threatened by global warming.

10   9   8   7   6

DANGERS OF GLOBAL WARMING

AL GORE BELIEVES GLOBAL WARMING IS HAPPENING MUCH FASTER THAN PEOPLE ANTICIPATE. CHECK OUT THIS PHOTO ESSAY TO SEE THE POTENTIAL DANGERS.

Fuels burned by cars and factories produce greenhouse gases. These gases rise and trap the sun's energy around Earth, creating a greenhouse effect.

Warmer weather causes bacteria to grow and disease-carrying insects to multiply. This may lead to an increased spread in infectious diseases and health problems.

infectious: *easily transferred to others*

The rise in temperature causes damaging storms and droughts that will seriously affect agriculture and lead to food shortages.

Warmer temperatures are causing glaciers to melt. During the past 100 years, sea levels have risen four to eight inches, resulting in erosion of sandy beaches and loss of land. Coastal nations such as Bangladesh are being flooded, forcing millions of people from their homes.

Take Note

Al Gore continues to travel the world, speaking about global warming. His speech provided an important message and challenged Americans to become more environmentally friendly. For his powerful words, Gore is #4 on our list.
• Do some research on global warming. Do you agree with Gore's fears? Should the government take more action in preventing global warming? Explain your answers.

5   **4**   3   2   1

In recognition of her work for women, Susan B. Anthony was depicted on the silver dollar in 1979. She was the first woman to be honored on a U.S. coin.

PERSONS?"

SUSAN B. ANTHONY—BETTMANN/CORBIS/ BE061463; WOMEN WITH BANNER—LIBRARY OF CONGRESS/LC-USZ62-95442; AMERICAN FLAG–ISTOCKPHOTO

WHO: Susan B. Anthony, women's rights activist

WHERE AND WHEN: Monroe and Ontario Counties, New York, January to June 1873

SIGNIFICANCE: Anthony's words rallied women to carry on the fight for the right to vote.

At the beginning of the 20th century, women still did not have suffrage, the right to vote!

For most of her life, Susan B. Anthony fought for this right. She made speeches, took part in rallies and protest marches, and lobbied politicians. She even practiced civil disobedience — an act in which a person breaks a law as a form of protest.

In the 1872 election, Anthony voted illegally and was arrested. She was found guilty at her trial in June 1873 and ordered to pay a fine of $100. Anthony refused, saying to the judge, "May it please your honor, I will never pay a dollar of your unjust penalty."

Anthony made her speech many times after her arrest and in the months preceding her trial. She began by using words from the Constitution, "It was we, the people; not we, the white male citizens; nor yet we, the male citizens; but we, the whole people, who formed the Union."

She then quoted the 14th Amendment to the Constitution, which states that "All persons born or naturalized in the United States … are citizens of the United States."

And she concluded by asking: "The only question left to be settled now is: Are women persons? I scarcely believe any of our opponents will … say they are not."

lobbied: *tried to influence*

"ARE WOMEN PERSONS?"

THE SPEAKER

Susan B. Anthony (1820–1906) grew up in a family of strong activists who believed in equal rights for men and women. The family also supported the antislavery and temperance (fight to ban alcohol) movements. In 1852, Anthony was refused the right to speak at a temperance rally because she was a woman. She turned her attention to woman suffrage and soon became a leader of the movement. In 1869, Anthony and her friend Elizabeth Cady Stanton formed the National Woman Suffrage Association to fight for a constitutional amendment that would give women the right to vote.

THE MOMENT

In the months before her trial, Anthony traveled around Monroe and Ontario Counties in western New York giving her speech. Her passionate words won cheers from her supporters.

THE IMPACT

Anthony's bold actions and words won her the support of other women. They too went out and made speeches and handed out petitions. Even some men began to admire her and to show their support. Unfortunately, Anthony died in 1906 without seeing her dream come true. It was not until 1920 that Congress passed the 19th Amendment of the Constitution, giving women the right to vote: "The right of a citizen of the United States to vote shall not be denied … on account of sex."

---

petitions: *formal written requests for action*

? Find out what happened in the struggle for suffrage after Susan B. Anthony's death. Why did it take another 14 years before the 19th Amendment was passed?

Quick Fact

In 1870, the 15th Amendment to the U.S. Constitution was passed, giving African American men, but not women, the right to vote.

Women celebrate the passing of the 19th Amendment in Washington, D.C., in August 1920.

10   9   8   7   6

"FAILURE IS IMPOSSIBLE"

In the early 20th century, women did not have many rights in the United States. Here's a list of the inequalities that women lived with.

- Women did not have the right to vote.
- Women could not file a lawsuit or sit on a jury.
- Women could not make a speech in public.
- Women were not admitted to colleges or universities.
- Women were not allowed to hold certain jobs, especially in business, medicine, and law.
- If a woman did have a job, she made one-quarter of what a man earned for the same work.
- If woman was married, a woman's employer gave her salary to her husband.
- The husband had the legal right to strike his wife.
- In a divorce, the father always had custody of the children.

At her 86th birthday celebration, Susan B. Anthony thanked the women who had devoted themselves to the struggle for equal rights: "With such women consecrating their lives, failure is impossible!" The last three words became a motto for thousands of women. They wrote them on banners and chanted them in marches and rallies.

consecrating: *devoting*

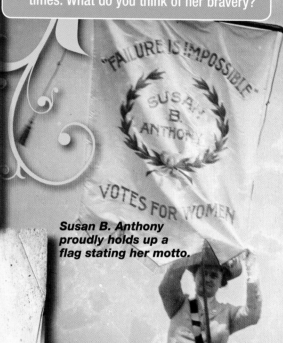

? Women were not allowed to make a speech in public, yet Anthony did so many times. What do you think of her bravery?

Susan B. Anthony proudly holds up a flag stating her motto.

The Expert Says...

" Anthony's ... words became the watchwords driving the long struggle for women's right to vote. Only the vote gives the power to protect one's rights. Today these words inspire all who seek equality. "

— Colleen Hurst, Historian, Susan B. Anthony House, Rochester, New York

Take Note

Anthony's defiant speech rings in at #3. Without the work of Susan B. Anthony, Nancy Pelosi might not be where she is today as Speaker of the House of Representatives. Anthony stirred strong emotions and significantly influenced the suffrage movement.
- The 19th Amendment is called the Susan B. Anthony Amendment. Find out about another struggle for rights that resulted in an amendment to the Constitution. What are the similarities and differences between the two movements?

5   4   **3**   2   1

King was born Michael Luther King but later changed his name to Martin, after a 15th century German monk, Martin Luther. King became a preacher and dedicated his life to religion, much like the German monk he admired.

...DREAM ..."

...that my four little children will one day live in a nation where they will not be judged

WHO: Martin Luther King Jr., civil rights activist

WHERE AND WHEN: Lincoln Memorial, Washington, D.C., August 28, 1963

SIGNIFICANCE: King's stirring speech moved his listeners to join the fight for equal rights for all Americans.

President Abraham Lincoln ended slavery in 1865. But 100 years later, much of America was still segregated into black and white worlds.

In the 1950s, Dr. Martin Luther King Jr. became the leader of the fight for rights for African Americans. Instead of violence, he urged peaceful demonstrations. King was an inspiring speaker. He was able to express clearly and movingly the demands of African Americans for equality.

In August 1963, King led a peaceful protest march to Washington, D.C. In front of a crowd of about 250,000 people, King delivered his most memorable speech: "I have a dream that one day this nation will rise up and live out the true meaning of its creed: 'We hold these truths to be self-evident, that all men are created equal …'

"I have a dream that my four little children will one day live in a nation where they will not be judged by the color of their skin but by the content of their character."

This stirring speech, delivered passionately and eloquently, became the foundation of the civil rights movement. It won worldwide attention for King and his mission.

creed: system of beliefs

by the color of their skin

"I HAVE A DREAM..."

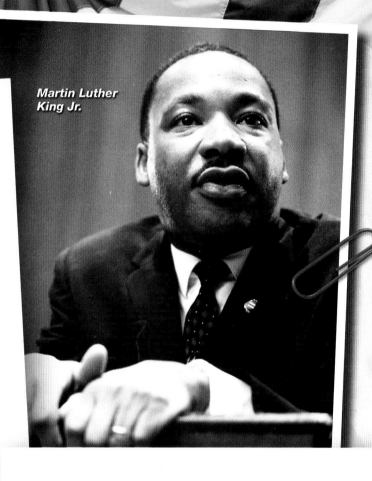

Martin Luther King Jr.

THE SPEAKER

Martin Luther King Jr. (1929 – 1968) was born in Atlanta, Georgia, to a family of ministers. A brilliant student, he followed his father's path and became a minister. As a leader of the civil rights movement, his stirring speeches and nonviolent protests won him millions of supporters, both black and white. In 1964, he was awarded the Nobel Peace Prize for his leadership in nonviolent civil rights demonstrations.

King made many enemies — many white people hated his ideas of equality. He was jailed many times. In 1968, at the age of 39, King was assassinated. He was shot on the balcony of the Lorraine Motel in Memphis, Tennessee. The motel is now the site of the National Civil Rights Museum.

> Even though they were born almost 100 years apart, King and Susan B. Anthony both struggled for equal rights for Americans. In what ways were they similar? How were they different?

The Expert Says...

" With words as his only weapon, the Reverend Dr. Martin Luther King Jr. communicated to his audience his passion and his vision of a just, peaceful society built on Christian values and the principles of the U.S. Constitution. He galvanized massive support for the powerful, peaceful Civil Rights Movement which shook American society for years to come. "

— Dr. M. G. Slavenas, Professor of Modern Languages, Canisius College, Buffalo, New York

galvanized: *stirred up*

THE MOMENT

From the steps of the Lincoln Memorial, King spoke to the largest turnout of protestors ever recorded in American history. Millions more watched on television. Because of the tension between King and his opponents, President John F. Kennedy ordered armed guards to stand in the crowd, in case of violence.

THE IMPACT

The March on Washington was given wide coverage by the media. King's stirring words had a huge impact on the nation. Less than a year later, in July 1964, Congress passed the Civil Rights Act. It banned segregation in public places and called for equal opportunities for blacks in employment and education.

Quick Fact

King is only one of only three Americans whose birthday is a national holiday. The other two people are George Washington and Abraham Lincoln, who are honored on Presidents' Day.

POWER
to the People!

The March on Washington was the most famous of the peaceful demonstrations organized by Dr. Martin Luther King Jr. — but it wasn't the only one. Check out some of his other successful protests in this fact chart.

Montgomery ...

When Rosa Parks was arrested in 1955 for not giving her bus seat to a white man, King called for the African Americans of Montgomery, Alabama, to boycott the bus system. The African American community banded together and they refused to ride in buses. The transportation system started losing lots of money. More than a year later, the boycott finally ended after the Supreme Court put an end to separate seating.

Birmingham ...

In 1963, King led huge demonstrations in Birmingham, Alabama, one of the most segregated cities in the South. The police turned dogs and fire hoses on the peaceful demonstrators. Widespread media reports of the police violence resulted in a public outcry. Soon after the protests, President John F. Kennedy proposed an important civil rights bill to Congress.

Selma ...

In 1965, King led demonstrations against efforts to stop African Americans from voting in elections. During a peaceful march from Selma, Alabama, to Montgomery, police used tear gas and clubs to break up the demonstrators. Televised footage shocked the nation. This led President Johnson to propose a bill to end voting discrimination, which Congress passed in 1965.

Take Note

Dr. Martin Luther King Jr.'s powerful speech stands at #2. It helped change American laws and attitudes. Like Susan B. Anthony, he made America a different nation by giving a voice to millions of Americans who felt silenced.
• Dr. Martin Luther King Jr. fought hard for his strong beliefs in civil rights, and he tried to do it peacefully. What do you think nonviolent protests can accomplish? How are nonviolent protests more effective than violent ones? Explain your answers.

" ... GOVERNME

Lincoln believed that
slavery was an evil.

NT OF THE PEOPLE ..."

WHO: Abraham Lincoln, president, 1861–1865

WHERE AND WHEN: Gettysburg National Cemetery, Pennsylvania, November 19, 1863

SIGNIFICANCE: Lincoln honored those who died in the Battle of Gettysburg and emphasized the need for the United States to come together as a nation.

The American Civil War started in 1861 when the Southern states that supported slavery and wanted to preserve states' rights separated from the United States. They created the Confederate States of America. President Abraham Lincoln vowed to preserve the Union. The Civil War would be the bloodiest in American history and last until 1865. The deadliest battle of the war was the Battle of Gettysburg in 1863. More Southerners than Northerners died in this battle. As a result, the South retreated, but the war continued until April 9, 1865.

The small town of Gettysburg became the resting place for 7,500 soldiers who were killed in the Battle of Gettysburg. At a ceremony to honor the dead, President Lincoln called on the country to unite. His famous speech became known as the *Gettysburg Address*. "We are met on a great battlefield of that war. We have come to dedicate a portion of that field as a final resting place for those who here gave their lives that that nation might live. It is altogether fitting and proper that we should do this."

Lincoln's speech lasted only two minutes, but it was one of the most powerful speeches in American history. He described the Battle of Gettysburg as "a new birth of freedom" and he stressed the importance of America as a nation. In his short speech, Lincoln captured the democratic ideals that all the other Americans on our list worked to enrich and to preserve.

"... GOVERNMENT OF THE PEOPLE ..."

THE SPEAKER

Lincoln grew up on a farm and had little formal schooling. He educated himself by reading constantly. He started with the Bible and the works of William Shakespeare and other famous English writers. He served briefly in the army and practiced as a lawyer. He also became interested in politics. He served in the Illinois legislature for four terms, from 1834 to 1841. In 1846, he was elected to the U.S. House of Representatives. He joined the Republican Party, which opposed slavery, and was elected president in 1860.

On April 14, 1865, Lincoln was shot and killed at Ford's Theatre in Washington, D.C. The assassin was John Wilkes Booth, an actor.

THE MOMENT

Lincoln delivered his speech during the dedication of the Gettysburg National Cemetery. It was four months after the Battle of Gettysburg. Fifteen thousand spectators were present. Lincoln's short speech came after one made by Edward Everett, a famous speaker, who spoke for two hours.

THE IMPACT

At the time, Lincoln's speech got little reaction from the crowd, but today it is regarded as one of the most eloquent in American history. Lincoln referred to the Declaration of Independence and its ideals of liberty and equality. He emphasized that the Civil War and the Battle of Gettysburg were fought for the reunification of the United States. The reunification would now require the efforts and sacrifices of all Americans. Lincoln died a month before the Civil War ended and he did not live to see the country reunited.

Quick Fact

There were over 51,000 casualties at the Battle of Gettysburg, making it the bloodiest battle of the Civil War. More than 600,00 people died in total during the Civil War.

? Why was the Battle of Gettysburg so significant? Research to find out.

The Battle of Gettysburg

The Expert Says...

" I can think of no one in literary or political history quite like this essential American writer [Lincoln]. "

— Gore Vidal, author of *Lincoln*

essential: *important*

10   9   8   7   6

Words of Wisdom

Abraham Lincoln was a powerful and eloquent speaker. Read an excerpt from his Gettysburg speech below to discover his beliefs and his way with words.

Four score and seven years ago our fathers brought forth on this continent, a new nation, conceived in Liberty, and dedicated to the proposition that all men are created equal.

Now we are engaged in a great civil war, testing whether that nation, or any nation so conceived and so dedicated, can long endure. We are met on a great battlefield of that war. We have come to dedicate a portion of that field as a final resting place for those who here gave their lives that that nation might live. …

The world will little note, nor long remember what we say here, but it can never forget what they did here. It is for us the living, rather, to be dedicated here to the unfinished work which they who fought here have thus far so nobly advanced. It is rather for us to be here dedicated to the great task remaining before us — that from these honored dead we take increased devotion to that cause for which they gave the last full measure of devotion — that we here highly resolve that these dead shall not have died in vain — that this nation, under God, shall have a new birth of freedom — and that government of the people, by the people, for the people, shall not perish from the earth.

proposition: *belief; intention*
endure: *survive*
nobly: *graciously*

resolve: *decide*
perish: *die*

? How do you think such a short and precise speech gained momentum over time?

Take Note

America's 16th president, Abraham Lincoln, is one of America's greatest leaders. The *Gettysburg Address* inspired generations of Americans and is our choice for the top spot on our list of greatest speeches.
- Do you agree that the *Gettysburg Address* deserves to be #1 on our list? Why or why not?

5   4   3   2   1

We Thought …

Here are the criteria we used in ranking the 10 most memorable speeches.

The speech:
- Stirred strong emotions in listeners
- Was given by an influential person
- Had enormous power
- Provided an important message
- Had an impact on America
- Was inspirational
- Calmed people's fears
- Brought about significant change
- Influenced history
- Is remembered by many

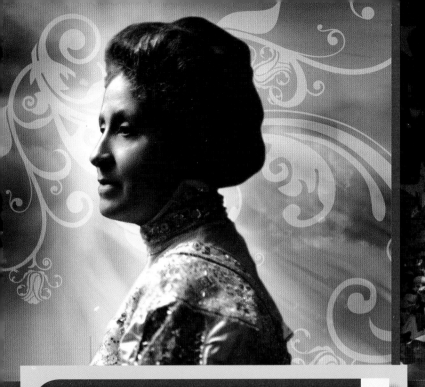

What Do You Think?

1. Do you agree with our ranking? If you don't, try ranking these speeches yourself. Justify your ranking with data from your own research and reasoning. You may refer to our criteria, or you may want to draw up your own list of criteria.

2. Here are three other speeches that we considered but in the end did not include in our top 10 list: *Bob Hope Humanitarian Award Acceptance Speech,* by Oprah Winfrey, on September 22, 2002, *Farewell to Baseball Address,* by Lou Gehrig, on July 4, 1939, and *The Struggle for Human Rights,* by Eleanor Roosevelt, on September 28, 1948.

   • Find out more about them. Do you think they should have made our list? Give reasons for your response.
   • Are there other speeches that you think should have made our list? Explain your choices.

Index